CHINESE STEAM
THE LAST YEARS

David Kitching

AMBERLEY

First published 2017

Amberley Publishing
The Hill, Stroud
Gloucestershire, GL5 4EP

www.amberley-books.com

Copyright © David Kitching, 2017

The right of David Kitching to be identified as
the Author of this work has been asserted in
accordance with the Copyright, Designs and
Patents Act 1988.

ISBN 978 1 4456 7620 3 (print)
ISBN 978 1 4456 7621 0 (ebook)

British Library Cataloguing in Publication Data.
A catalogue record for this book is available from
the British Library.

Origination by Amberley Publishing.
Printed in the UK.

Photographing Chinese Steam Locomotives in Action

By the 1990s, it was becoming clear to enthusiasts that China was the one place where steam locomotives were likely to survive in significant numbers for some time. The country had opened up to visitors significantly and many formerly closed areas were now available. Not only was there the lure of steam, but also the opportunity to visit areas that no package holidays were ever likely to feature, and to meet people from a very different culture.

Although I had not been particularly active in the pursuit of steam since it ended in Britain on the main line in 1968 and subsequently faded away in industry, I had maintained an interest through the railway press. As stories of adventures in China began to filter back, along with some splendid photographs of exotic locomotives and locations, I became determined to see a bit of this for myself. This resulted in a trip to the north-east of China in 1992, which featured a significant amount of main line steam activity as well as visits to coal mines, steelworks, locomotive works and even a narrow-gauge logging line. This was followed by a series of trips that were first prompted by the opening of the Jitong Railway across the Mongolian Autonomous Region, which started as 100 per cent steam operated.

There were still lots of industrial lines to visit in the mid-2000s, including a few narrow-gauge operations. After visiting a good number on organised group trips, I ventured into freelance visits along with two or three friends, and sometimes joined by my son, Tom. By securing the services of a specialist guide who knew what we required, these trips were made very easy to achieve. There are a number of steam tour guides in China and we were lucky in that we chose to use Ma Junming, who is better known to enthusiasts as Mike Ma. Thanks to Mike we never missed a train we needed to catch or a flight to some remote region. There was always a minibus awaiting us on arrival at distant steelworks towns and a decent hotel to catch up on sleep after a long, cold day in the desert. Mike also ensured we always had the required permits for the lines that required them before visitors were allowed to take photographs. He never let us down and saved us from the inevitable complications and hassles involved in booking long-distance rail tickets in China.

Many of the trips were made in winter, when the exhaust from steam locomotives was at its most spectacular. Of course, in the north-east of China this meant very low temperatures, which were often made far worse by the windchill factor. Waiting for trains at -25°C in a steady wind blowing from Siberia soon made you long for a warm restaurant and taught you to keep moving. The dry cold was manageable with several layers of clothing, balaclavas and furry hats, plus handwarmers inside two layers of gloves. The lowest temperature we experienced was -40°C at Jalainur, when cameras ceased to function after only a minute or two when removed from under my coat. Frostbite was always a danger at these temperatures and your breath soon formed an icy layer on your eyebrows, and there was a tendency for the camera to freeze to your nose when taking a picture! Having said all that, I did enjoy most of the time out in the cold, and the steam effects from the locomotives made it all worthwhile.

As the years went by it was expected that steam would soon end in China. Indeed, the Chinese government was said to want old-fashioned steam trains to be gone by the time the Olympic Games were held in Beijing in 2008. This did not happen and while the numbers of steam operations was falling rapidly, a few kept going and previously unknown industrial steam sites continued to be discovered occasionally. Even as I write in 2017, there is still steam in operation at a small number of locations, but this is usually just the odd locomotive shunting and it is unlikely that much will survive for much longer (apart from the narrow-gauge line at Shibanxi, which seems to be making the transition to a tourist steam railway). Judging by the numbers of Chinese people that are now using its services just for fun it may well flourish indefinitely. A further narrow-gauge line, the Yujian Railway in Henan Province, reopened as a tourist attraction in May 2017 and has six steam locomotives available for services.

The locomotives featured in this book are nearly all QJ Class 2-10-2, JS Class 2-8-2 and SY Class 2-8-2 standard-gauge locomotives. On the narrow gauge, the C2 Class 0-8-0 ruled on all the lines that I visited and had a gauge of 2 feet 6 inches (762 mm).

If you want to see and learn more, there is a vast range of video of Chinese steam in action on websites such as YouTube. Duncan Cotterill's Railography website (www.railography.co.uk/info/info.htm) contains a wealth of detail about the history and allocation of Chinese standard-gauge steam locomotives as well as a range of useful maps of the main locations. For details of visits to Chinese steam railways from 2000 to date see the SY Country website (www.sy-country.co.uk/qjc/content.htm).

Further reading

These are a selection of the books that cover various aspects of Chinese steam locomotives and railways:

Adley, R., *To China for Steam* (Poole: Blandford Press, 1983).

Clark, P., *Locomotives in China* (Waterloo, NSW: Roundhouse Press, 1983).

Garratt, C., *China's Railways: Steaming Into a New Age* (Wellingborough: Patrick Stephens, 1988).

le Cheminant, S., Murphy, R., Rhodes, M., *Extreme Steam* (Carnforth: Tele Rail Publications, 2000).

le Cheminant, S., Murphy, R., Rhodes, M., *21st Century Extreme Steam* (Carnforth: Tele Rail Publications, 2003).

Pritchard, R.N., *Industrial Locomotives of the People's Republic of China* (2nd ed., Melton Mowbray: Industrial Railway Society, 2008).

Tickner, J., Edgar, G., Freeman, A., *China: The World's Last Steam Railway* (Wisley: Artists' and Photographers' Press Ltd, 2008).

Whitehouse, P. B., *China's Railways: Today's Image* (Edgbaston: Millbrook House Ltd, 1986).

Whitehouse, P. B., Whitehouse, M., *China by Rail* (London: Century Hutchinson Ltd, 1988).

Acknowledgements

I feel privileged to have been able to visit so many places and railways in China and this would not have been possible without the help and organisation of my good friend Ma Junming. Thanks are due for the tours organised by Andy Clarke and the late Ron Lingley, and also Bernd Seiler, whose FarRail Tours always deliver superb photographic opportunities. There have been so many congenial travelling companions but special thanks to David Hill who has patiently tried to teach me to improve my photographic skills on these trips, and also to Andrew Fewster, Alan Murray-Rust and Tom Kitching for helping to make the visits so much fun. Finally, my appreciation of the Chinese people, who made us very welcome and were prepared to humour the strange requests to visit mines and other industries that to them probably held no interest or attraction beyond being a place of employment.

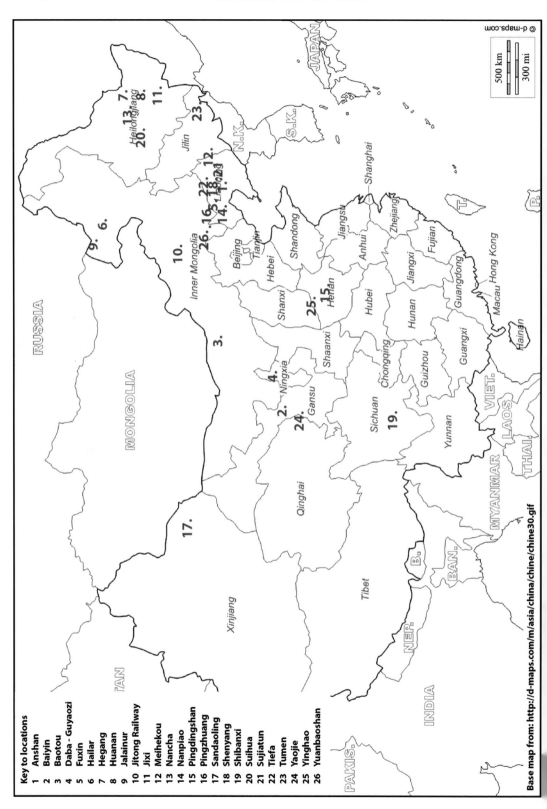

Key to locations
1 Anshan
2 Baiyin
3 Baotou
4 Daba - Guyaozi
5 Fuxin
6 Hailar
7 Hegang
8 Huanan
9 Jalainur
10 Jitong Railway
11 Jixi
12 Meihekou
13 Nancha
14 Nanpiao
15 Pingdingshan
16 Pingzhuang
17 Sandaoling
18 Shenyang
19 Shibanxi
20 Suihua
21 Sujiatun
22 Tiefa
23 Tumen
24 Yaojie
25 Yinghao
26 Yuanbaoshan

Base map from: http://d-maps.com/m/asia/china/chine/chine30.gif

QJ No. 2712 outside the roundhouse at Hailar having just arrived on a freight from the Harbin direction. This depot was very busy, with the turntable in almost constant use. (14 October 1992).

QJ No. 2758 has just backed on to a westbound freight in Hailar station. A similar locomotive has brought the train in from the Russian border beyond Manzhouli and has departed for servicing at the nearby depot. The QJs in this area were built in the 1970s with four-axle tenders, which were adequate for the length of runs expected of them. (14 October 1992).

Diesels were only just beginning to make an appearance at Suihua in October 1992. It is Sunday morning at the shed preparation area and there is non-stop steam action. (18 October 1992).

At this time the rail services at Suihua were nearly all steam operated and most trains changed locomotives here. QJ No. 6843 backs down to a train in Suihua station while pilots JS No. 5693 and JS No. 5740 shunt the freight yard and remove empty stock from the platform respectively. (18 October 1992).

Naming railway locomotives is not a great tradition in China. However, there have been occasions where locomotives have been chosen to be specially decorated and named. In these cases there were no half measures and the locomotives were kept in splendid external condition. While linesiding at Suihua, QJ No. 6800 passed with a heavy coal train. This locomotive was named *Iron Bull* (*Tieniu Hao*) and was the favourite of the Suihua depot. It has survived and was plinthed at Jixi diesel depot. (18 October 1992).

QJ No. 6843 Heads north from Suihua with a long freight. Every few minutes another train would depart in this direction, destined either for the line to Bei'an and Fuyu or north-westward to Jiamusi, with some traffic branching north at Nancha for Wuyiling. The mixed nature of the loads carried is evident from the variety of wagons making up the train. (18 October 1992).

QI No. 6952 is seen here storming up the incredibly steep and curved southern side of Nancha bank. The train was banked by a second QI running tender first. The action on both sides of the summit made this area very popular for photography until diesels took over in 1994. (19 October 1992).

In 1992, one of the more spectacular steam locations was the steep climb up both sides of the bank at Nancha in Heilongjiang Province, on the branch to Wuyiling. A regular procession of trains loaded with timber would slowly ascend from Liushu with two QIs at the front and another banking. (19 October 1992).

The river bridge at Bi Shui provided excellent photographic opportunities in the morning. This view has long been lost due to a new road being built. Here, a QJ heads an early morning train from Tumen, on the border with North Korea, towards Dunhua and Jilin. (22 October 1992).

Vehicles queue at the toll booth on the main road out of Tumen as QJ No. 1130 passes with the 08.15 train to Jilin. Within a few years road traffic had expanded massively and this location now has a motorway through the middle. At this time, all the rail services in this area were steam operated. (22 October 1992).

Slag ladles on the move at the Anshan steelworks south of Shenyang. At the time we were told that the works employed around 250,000 people! It is certainly one of the largest steelworks in the world. (24 October 1992).

A Sunday afternoon spent at Hunhe Junction on the outskirts of Shenyang provided a feast of steam with a succession of heavy freights passing by. QJ No. 6487 was heading south away from Shenyang towards Sujiatun. This locomotive was built at Datong in 1983 and finished its working life in 2000. (25 October 1992).

A freight headed by local engine QJ No. 3286 passes over a small level crossing at busy Hunhe Junction. I had climbed up onto the overbridge carrying the Fushun line over the main line from Shenyang in order to get a good view over the station. The next train to appear comprised a number of flat wagons loaded with artillery pieces and troops, and the cameras were rapidly put away. (25 October 1992).

QJ Class 2-10-2 locomotives were normally fitted with smoke deflectors but those used for shunting duties or as yard pilot often had them removed for improved visibility. No. 3132 was one such when seen in the shed yard at Sujiatun, a short distance from Shenyang. (25 October 1992).

Sujiatun industrial locomotive works overhauled locomotives for a wide range of mines, steelworks, quarries and so on. Works shunter GJ No. 1018 is pulling an SY Class from the erecting shop while a further SY is undergoing a steam test on the left. In the 1990s tank engines were scarce in China and this was the only GJ that I ever saw in steam. (25 October 1992).

SY No. 1556 undergoing a steam test at the Sujiatun repair workshops. There were no cylinder ends on the locomotive and this was the result when the regulator was opened. (25 October 1992).

Baiyin

In Gansu Province, the Baiyin Mining Railway, operated by the Baiyin Nonferrous Metal (Group) Co. Ltd, serves mines and smelters for copper, zinc and lead. The main line runs for about 19 km from the town of Baiyinshi to the deep copper mine at Shenbutong via the zinc smelter at Sanyelian. At Baiyin Gongsi there are extensive sidings with branches to numerous tips and smelters, all of which add variety to the operations. Here, SY No. 0206 rushes the climb into the yard at Gongsi with a number of acid tanks. In the background stands the shot tower at the lead smelter. (19 January 2006).

SY No. 1583 with the morning empties to the Kuangsan copper mine. This train runs every day after the morning passenger service has returned from the mine, although the exact timing is difficult to predict as it can appear at any time over a period of about four hours. Luckily, on this day there was enough time to climb the hills overlooking the line, but not so much that I was standing in the cold for very long. (4 December 2009).

SY No. 1583 hammers uphill towards Shenbutong on the Baiyin Mining Railway with empties for the Kuangsan copper mine at the top of the line. The uphill trains on this line are regularly worked with the locomotives flat out and at the limits of adhesion. This train made a wonderful sound with the noise of the exhaust bouncing off the surrounding hills. (20 January 2006).

The morning passenger service to Shenbutong copper mine runs before sunrise in midwinter but still offers plenty of scenic opportunity. The plaque on the front of SY No. 2008 was to celebrate the Beijing Olympics of 2008. (5 December 2009).

A few minutes before the sun crept over the edge of the mountains, SY No. 2008 hurries the morning passenger service towards Shenbutong. This locomotive was renumbered from 0701 in honour of the Olympic year and was the first train of my 2009 visit to China. (4 December 2009).

Baotou

At Baotou, in the Mongolian Autonomous Region, is an extensive steelworks that used steam locomotives until the end of 2008. The blast furnaces dominate the background to the locomotive preparation yard as SY No. 1431 prepares to go to work. (6 December 2006).

SY No. 1431 simmers at the servicing point among piles of ash and clinker. The coaling conveyor rises from the left. (8 December 2008).

With only three weeks to go to the end of steam, repairs continued to be undertaken in the workshops at Baotou. (8 December 2008).

SY No. 1727 shunts among the furnaces and slag pots. (8 December 2008).

The extensive slag banks at Baotou provided the sight of slag being tipped from the pots. The light on the drifting steam was worth waiting for in this case and lasted for just a few seconds. (6 December 2006).

Hot, solid slag was also tipped from the pots on the banks. The SY on this duty is just visible through the heat haze rising from the slag. (6 December 2006).

Guyaozi

QJ No. 7200 is well on its way to Daba as it crosses the frozen Yellow River on the Daba to Guyaozi line in Ningxia Hui Autonomous Region. This line runs for 70 km, linking coal mines and chemical works in the desert to the main line at Daba. (17 January 2006).

The extension of the railway to the new coal mine at Yangchangwan was only completed in 2005. Until the diesels took over at the end of 2006, QJ Class locomotives hauled long trains through the desert to and from Guyaozi. There wasn't much sun around on this visit and the temperature was below freezing. (17 January 2006).

Steam on a new line; QJ No. 7036 works a long train of empties towards the coal mine at Yangchangwan, which opened in 2005. In the background are coal-loading facilities close to the junction with the branch to the mine at Lingxingkuang. (18 January 2006).

The visit to the desert line between Daba and Guyaozi was intended to make shots amidst the dunes and wide open spaces. The weather had other ideas and the falling snow soon reduced visibility and required a change of tactics. QJ No. 7205 is seen nearing Guyaozi with a long train of empty coal wagons. (18 January 2006).

As the snow set in there was no choice but to brave the low light and lack of visibility. QJ No. 7205 was captured across the cemetery as it passed the intermediate town of Lingwu. Diesels took over within months. (18 January 2006).

East of Lingwu the railway passes through a desert and semi-desert landscape all the way to the mines at Guyaozi. After a long wait on a bleak hillside the afternoon empties arrived behind QJ No. 7194, which was thrashing uphill in great style. (17 January 2006).

Fuxin

The Fuxin Mining Administration in Liaoning Province operated an extensive network linking coal mines to the main line and also serving a power station. The large fleet of SY Class locomotives was maintained in this large workshop, where one dismantled locomotive can be seen. (28 September 2004).

The waiting traffic at this level crossing in Fuxin occupies the whole width of the roadway. Of course, a similar situation is to be found on the other side of the tracks, and things will become interesting once the barriers are slid aside. (29 September 2004).

Steam locomotives and bicycles go together in China. This driver in Fuxin has ensured that his personal transport will be available wherever he finishes his shift. (28 September 2004).

Fuxin had several crossings in the town, where the locals paid little attention as the locomotives went about their daily work. Steam working finished at the end of August 2016. (28 September 2004).

SY No. 0941 shunts coal while one of the overhead-wire electric locomotives handles a load of spoil for the Wulong tip. The electric locomotives were out of use by 2007, with their duties taken over by steam. (28 September 2004).

There was also a regular local passenger service and a number of miners' paddy trains run on the system. A westbound passenger service is seen here passing Wulong Yard, near the main power station. (28 September 2004).

Hegang

The Hegang Mining Railway serves a number of collieries and a power station and was partly electrified, although steam trains ran throughout the system, including the regular passenger service. A morning service is seen here departing from Fuli mine as miners trudge to work along an electrified narrow-gauge line. (11 April 2005).

One of the main traffic flows at Hegang is coal from the Fuli and Xingan mines to the Xinhua power station. Chimney-first operation to Xinhua was rare but in this case SY No. 0635 was leading with a heavy load of coal. (12 April 2005).

The morning passenger service from the outlying collieries is seen over the rooftops as it climbs the steep bank towards Dalu. The locomotive was reduced almost to a crawl by the time it crossed the summit. (11 April 2005).

SY No. 0635 works hard up the bank with coal hoppers for the power station at Xinhua. At this point the Hegang Coal Railway crosses over the China Rail main line to Hegang. (12 April 2005).

The old passes over the new. Regular passenger locomotive SY No. 1498 shortly after leaving Dalu with a morning passenger service. The diesel is on the National Railways' main line and luckily was in just the right position when the other train ran over the bridge. (27 November 2006).

On a cold, murky morning, SY No. 1498 accelerates away from Dalu mine, which can be seen in the background. The overhead wires were only used by electric locomotives hauling coal trains from Fuli into Hegang. (28 November 2006).

Huanan Coal Railway

There were once extensive networks of narrow-gauge railways in China serving forestry extraction, mines and brickworks. By the early years of the twentieth century these had dwindled to just a few lines, mainly moving coal until the traffic ended or was replaced by lorries. A favourite line was the Huanan Coal Railway, which had been converted from forestry to coal traffic and ran several trains a day to and from the mine at Lixin. (30 November 2006).

The C2 Class 0-8-0 tender locomotives used on the narrow gauge could sound very loud when working hard. As a Lixin-bound train approaches the passing place at Xiahua, the noise of the train has frightened the motive power on the adjacent road and the drivers fight to keep control. (13 April 2005).

After Xiahua the Huanan line began a stiff climb over a range of hills, which were ascended via a series of looping curves before the final straight to the summit, where the locomotive was opened out. (14 April 2005).

West of Xiahua, towards Huanan, the line comprised a series of long straights across a fairly level plain. It passed through several small villages where livestock grazed very close to the tracks. (30 November 2006).

On the climb from Lixin to the summit, the loaded trains were banked by the locomotive off the previous load of empties. They still have a long way to go here to reach the summit, from where the banker will run back tender first to collect its own loaded train after the next load of empties has arrived. (29 November 2006).

The empty coal wagons are about halfway up the climb to the summit as the train passes the lineman's house, which adds a touch of colour to the scene. (14 April 2005).

Jalainur

Jalainur opencast mine was close to the Russian border in the Mongolian Autonomous Region of China. It was sometimes possible to see twenty SY Class locomotives in action at one time. (4 December 2006).

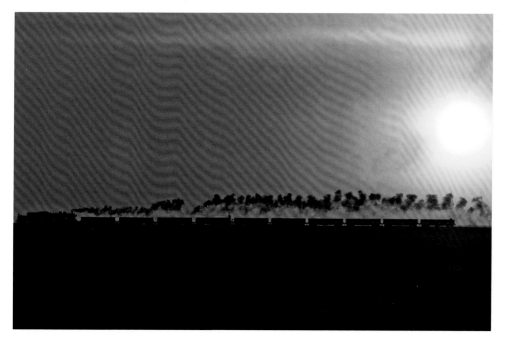

Jalainur mine is a cold and often windy place in winter. On this occasion, while cold it was also still, and as the sun set a train running on the dirt tip at Nanzhan was silhouetted with a perfect steam exhaust running the length of the wagons. (4 December 2006).

Sometimes you get double value in a photograph and this shot from within the opencast pit at Jalainur demonstrates a two-tier approach. (19 January 2008).

The two morning passenger services into the Jalainur opencast mine were combined for the return trip on this morning. Sometimes they would come separately with the second one pushing out. (20 January 2006).

The use of smoke deflectors on the SY Class locomotives was uncommon and completely changed their look. SY No. 1416 is seen at Jalainur washery, as the only locomotive so fitted on this system. (2 December 2006).

The late afternoon sun glints on the bucket of the electric shovel on the Jalainur dirt tips. SY No. 1678 provides the steam action. (4 December 2006).

Jitong Railway

A heavy westbound freight crosses the Reshui viaduct at sunrise. I waited at this location for four days before a train came at the right moment. The 945-km Jitong railway between Jining and Tongliao in the Mongolian Autonomous Region opened in 1995 and was the last main line railway in the world to use steam locomotives. (5 October 2004).

Westbound freight is seen between Linxi and Reshui, from where it will begin the sinuous ascent of the Jingpeng section, which climbs both sides to a summit at Shangdian. The gradient is such that double-heading was the norm between Daban and Haloukou. (21 April 2004).

Two QJ Class locomotives climb across the curved viaduct at Simingyi as they haul an eastbound train towards the summit. For once the Jingpeng wind is pushing the exhaust away from the camera. (22 April 2004).

It is late afternoon as this eastbound train comes off the Simingyi viaduct. The spectacular scenery of this section is evident, as is the sinuous nature of the line, which can be seen curving back again across the valley from the train. (22 April 2004).

In the last months of steam operation on the Jitong Railway, a pair of QJs hurry a long freight into the station loops at Gulumanhan between Daban and Lindong. (22 April 2005).

By 2005 a new motorway was being built across the region and this opened up new opportunities for photography by using the unfinished road to access the line. This viaduct with a westbound train is towards Dariqiga on the section between Lindong and Daban. (17 April 2005).

Autumn is already creeping into the mountains around the Jingpeng section and the threshing of the harvest is well underway. A pair of QJs head a freight across the main road at San Di and onto the long looping climb towards Shangdian. (5 October 2004).

A fireman on the Jitong Railway ensures that lubrication is all in order on QJ No. 7081 during a stop at Lindong. The crews were invariably friendly and this chap shared his lunch with me when I went for a footplate ride on this train. (3 October 2004).

The exhaust hangs in the still air right around the curve as QJ No. 7038 approaches an accommodation crossing just outside Gulumanhan on the morning of my last day on the Jitong Railway. (23 April 2005).

Semaphore signals abound at the passing places on the Jitong line. This is the eastern end of Gulumanhan, where a westbound train is entering the loops. (17 April 2005).

Daban was the location of a major locomotive depot and the workshops for the line. Locomotives were changed here and a fresh pair of QJs are seen departing the yard, heading east. (21 April 2005).

A mass of locomotives in steam and a steam coaling crane seen in the yard at Daban depot. There was a steady procession of locomotives in and out via the turning triangle. (4 October 2004).

The eastbound passenger service departs from Chaganhada soon after sunrise. Regular locomotive, QJ No. 6911, is in charge. This was the last regular long-distance, main line, steam-hauled passenger service in the world. (21 April 2005).

The wide open spaces on the approaches to Lindong are typical of this section of the line. This short train will soon loop round to pass to the right of the photographer. (22 April 2005).

It is just after 6 a.m. and westbound QJs No. 7048 and No. 7012 reach the summit soon after leaving Chaganhada, from where it was then downhill to Daban. A few months later, scenes such as this were gone forever. (23 April 2005).

Westbound from Chabuga towards Lindong are QJs No. 7119 and No. 6977 and a load of tanker wagons. This was the last photo of the day even though it was only midday, as the line seemed to go into suspended animation with no trains until after dark. It was a frustrated bunch of photographers that arrived back at the hotel that evening. (20 April 2005).

Having photographed this train further down the valley shortly after it had left Jingpeng, we pursued it to try to get a shot from the hillside above the brickworks viaduct at Er Di. Unfortunately, we found ourselves behind a slow motorbike on the bumpy track to the viaduct, and all the time I could see the train getting nearer. I just had time to jump out of the bus and press the shutter. I am now glad that I didn't have time to climb the hill as this is one of my favourite shots from the Jingpeng section. (7 October 2004).

A little glint as QJs No. 6751 and No. 6876 cross Jingpeng west viaduct and head into the sunset with a westbound freight soon after leaving the station at Jingpeng. (6 October 2004).

The millet is being loaded from the fields as a QJ heads west towards Lindong and the farmers pay little attention to the passing train. (3 October 2004).

Glorious afternoon light catches an eastbound freight just after leaving the Simingyi viaduct on the Jingpeng section of the Jitong railway. A few tunnels and a steep climb and then they will be able to coast down towards Reshui. (22 April 2004).

Jixi – Chengzihe

There are five separate lines connecting collieries to the national rail network around Jixi. The largest and busiest of these is the Chengzihe system. A regular visit was to the early morning shift change at Dongchang Colliery on the Chengzihe line. Sometimes there would be seven locomotives in the yard at the same time. (1 December 2006).

Typical gloomy Chinese winter conditions as a pair of SYs set out from the yard at Dongchang colliery with a long coal train, heading for the national railway interchange. (4 December 2008).

The collection of small pieces of coal and semi-coal from the waste material has been developed into a highly organised activity on the Xinghua colliery tips. Every trainload of material is sifted by the picking gangs who operate not only on the level summit area but also on the steep and dangerous slope on the other side of the tracks. (4 December 2008).

SY No. 1344 heads back to the Dongchang colliery from the exchange sidings at Jixi. Loaded trains tend to work across the bridge in the early morning and empties at night, so we were lucky to catch this light engine crossing on a bitterly cold afternoon. (25 November 2006).

It is late afternoon at the Beichang washery and for once all the locomotives are standing smokebox facing out. There was a steady stream of spoil trains running from here to the tips beyond Donchang. (6 December 2008).

A yard man signals for another locomotive to draw forward to the ash cleaning area in Nanchang Yard during the morning servicing break. The coal pickers stand on the ash wagon in the hope of rich rewards in a few minutes time. (25 November 2006).

The morning empty coal wagons to Xinghua colliery were combined with the empty spoil wagons on this particular morning. The first attempt to surmount the fierce bank out of Zhengyang ended in failure and, after rolling back down the hill, a spirited effort was made by both locomotives and the train was making steady progress when it passed where we stood on the Xinghua spoil banks. (16 December 2009).

An empty spoil train at the crossing just outside the Donchang colliery yard. The constant flow of coal and spoil trains over this crossing often caused large traffic queues in this part of the town. (4 December 2008).

With the wind whipping the exhaust away, the morning train of spoil tippers heads up from Zhengyang mine to the tip at Xinghua, where it will back up onto the mound. Since this photo was taken the line has been electrified. (14 December 2009).

It is early morning at the Nanchang servicing point with the crew emptying the ashpan and oiling around the locomotive. (6 January 2008).

Jixi – Didao

Shunting is seen at the Didao Hebei washery. The circular building contains a concentrator for dealing with coal slurry, which is then often used to make briquettes. It is roofed over because of the extreme cold experienced in the north-east of China in the winter. (25 November 2006).

Tipping small coal onto the massive pile at the tip by the Didao washery; it was a steep push up for SY No. 1213, but an easy roll back down once everything was empty. (14 December 2009).

The late afternoon sun catches SY No. 1205 hurrying across a level crossing as it brings a loaded coal train from the mines in the hills down to the washery at Didao. (17 December 2009).

Sometimes there was plenty to see at Didao as in this view, which shows a train returning from the power station on the left and another from the China Rail exchange sidings on the right. (7 December 2008).

Jixi – Donghaikuang

SY No. 0639 shunts alongside the Donghaikuang servicing area as a gleaner sorts through the ash pile. (3 December 2008).

It is a long and rough drive from the centre of Jixi town to this mine at Donghaikuang, which is situated on a remote section of the Jixi Coal Railway. Trains on this branch have to travel some distance over the National Railways to reach the combined heat and power plant at Jidong. There is usually only one train each way during daylight in winter and this is being prepared here, with much shunting under the distant loading bunkers. (3 December 2008).

Having waited for some time, the train to Jidong finally came into sight. There was much debate as to whether the line was uphill away from Donghaikuang colliery at this point and we soon learned that it was downhill as the train coasted past with just steam showing from the brake pump exhaust. The Donghaikuang mine can be seen in the background. (3 December 2008).

SY No. 0639 is hurrying a loaded train towards Jidong across this long viaduct on the Chinese National Railway line. We waited about an hour and a half in the biting wind to take this shot, having walked a long way from the nearest road crossing, but it was well worth it. (17 December 2009).

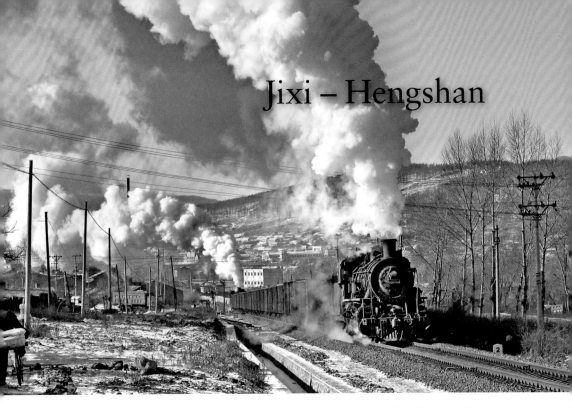

Jixi – Hengshan

The Hengshan system at Jixi serves a number of coal mines, which were reached by first ascending a steep bank that required banking of all but the lightest trains. Morning empties from the Hengshan exchange sidings were a favourite for photography. (22 November 2006).

There aren't many people who can say that they have seen a train of coaches ascending Hengshan bank on the Jixi Coal Railway. This particular working comprised two flat wagons loaded with concrete bridge sections, the Qiqihar-based crane and six coaches of its support train. SY 1369 headed the train banked by SY No. 1095 as they ran up the hill in fine style. (23 November 2006).

This photograph was a case of being in the right place at the right time. SYs No. 1369 and No. 1095 had brought the 160-ton capacity Qiqihar-based rail crane up the Hengshan bank with the final concrete beam for a new bridge close to the colliery at Zhangzin. (23 November 2006).

At the top of the Hengshan bank, a line reverses off to a colliery at Lijing. SY No. 1018, minus a lot of its chimney, is seen leaving the mine and enormous spoil tip with a loaded train. (7 December 2008).

Jixi – Lishu

SY No. 0477 stands in the yard at Xifeng on the Lishu system, which served several coal mines including one at the top of a steep branch. From here it was a short distance to the interchange with the National Railway network. (23 November 2006).

Loaded trains drifted down the Lishu line, as in this case with a load of coal from Pingan Mine. (5 December 2008).

SY No. 0951 crosses the river bridge on the approach to Lishu after loading the wagons at the nearby Taiping Mine at the junction with the branch that ran to Qikeng Mine. (15 December 2009).

We waited all afternoon for the injectors to be repaired on this locomotive, hoping that it would make the run to the Qikeng Mine before it became dark. The sun was already behind the hills when it finally came up the bank past the Sijing Cokeworks. The train had reversed just below the small colliery visible in the background. (23 November 2006).

SY No. 0477 was seen after leaving Xifeng with a train that included three wooden-bodied hopper wagons of a type that I never saw anywhere else in China. (23 November 2006).

At the distinctive pink and blue Pingang Mine on the Lishu system, SY No. 1118 sets out from under the bunkers with a long train. Loaded trains run downhill from Pingang on this line apart from the first few hundred metres, which climb from the bunkers past the traffic office, which is seen here on the right. (5 December 2008).

Meihekou

The Meihekou Coal Mining Administration in Jilin Province operates a railway connecting a number of collieries with workshops at Yijing (First) Mine. There is a branch that crosses this long viaduct and connects with the Chinese National Railway at Heishantou. (11 January 2006).

A youngster unconcernedly crosses the line just ahead of a loaded train bound for the exchange at Heishantou, heading away from the washery on the Meihekou Coal Railway. (11 January 2006).

SY No. 1662 starts its train after a stop by a road crossing to drop off miners who have just finished their nightshift at one of the Meihekou collieries. The exhaust illustrates just how cold it was that morning as we chased the train through the frozen countryside. (11 January 2006).

In the late afternoon on a desperately cold day, the sun is setting fast as SY No. 0791 hurries the empties towards Sanjing (Third) Mine. (11 January 2006).

Shunting at the throat of the yard at Yijing. Motorbike taxis wait for trade below the crossing. (11 January 2006).

On an extremely cold day, SY No. 1662 heads towards Sanjing Mine with a train of empty spoil tippers and coal hoppers. In the early morning the temperature fell off the bottom of our thermometer at -35°C. (11 January 2006).

Nanpiao

The Nanpiao Mine Railway in Liaoning Province comprises a main line that splits into two branches, with each serving a number of collieries. There is also a passenger service throughout. This is a service returning to Huangjia terminus, which is seen passing the depot outside Xiamiaozi. (10 January 2006).

The use of the railway as a pedestrian thoroughfare is normal practice across China; certainly nobody seems the slightest bit concerned that SY No. 1299 is on its way from the station at Huangjia with the afternoon passenger service on the Nanpiao Coal Railway. (10 January 2006).

There appeared to be no consistent traffic flow, with loaded and empty coal trains apparently running in all directions. Here we were sitting on a hilltop while waiting for the afternoon passenger service and were presented instead with a long train of empty coal wagons heading away from the washery and collieries, and towards the power station. (22 January 2008).

Every afternoon at around 3 p.m., two passenger services departed from Xiamiaozi. The first had come from Huangjia and was heading for Linghai while the other was the connecting service which then proceeded to Sanjiazi. (10 January 2006).

An afternoon passenger service to Sanjiazi climbs away from Fulongshan amidst the rolling hills typical of this part of Liaoning. These services were always well patronised by the local population. (22 January 2008).

The sun is rapidly setting as the afternoon passenger service to Linghai crosses the frozen river on its approach to Quiatou. (10 January 2006).

Pingdingshan

At Pingdingshan in Henan Province, the mining railway network was extensive and served collieries around the city, and also many kilometres away on the long main line of the system. Within the city there were several busy level crossings between Tianzhuang and Zhongxin. Before the crossings were replaced, JS No. 8054 attracts an audience as it approaches the central station at Zhongxin. (27 January 2006).

Darkness descends as deflectorless QJ No. 6650 arrives at Qilidian bringing coal from the distant mines at Yuzhou. (25 January 2006).

The passenger service passing right through the middle of various collieries is a feature of the Pingdingshan line. At colliery No. 7, the afternoon service to Baofeng points westwards and is making a grand show behind JS No. 8062. (27 January 2006).

On the line towards Baofeng we were able to chase JS No. 8338, which was running fast with empty coal hoppers. Our driver caught up with the train at an over bridge and I made this shot in the mist and murk that is typical of Pingdingshan in winter. (11 January 2008).

A winter morning shift change at Tianzhuang depot on the Pingdingshan Coal Railway. There was always a good line-up of JS locos at this time. (10 January 2008).

An early morning shift change at Tianzhuang shed on the Pingdingshan Coal Railway. The coal gleaners are hard at work as the JS Class locomotives pass over the ash pits and onto the servicing and water point. (27 January 2006).

Tianzhuang depot was at its busiest twice a day when the locomotives arrived for servicing. By this time it was one of the largest active steam depots in the world. (27 January 2006).

A loaded coal train from Yuzhou is seen crossing the river bridge at Xiancheng on the way towards Pingdingshan. I shall never forget the sound of the chime whistle as it approached the village crossings just beyond the bridge. One of the sand barges navigating the narrow ice-free river channel can be seen in the distance. (25 January 2006).

Morning activity as JS No. 5644 leaves Tianzhuang yard on the Pingdingshan Coal Railway with a long train of coal empties. (26 January 2006).

A JS hurries empty coal wagons towards the distant collieries on the long branch to the west of Baofeng. It is almost dark even though this is only just before 1 p.m. (11 January 2008).

JS No. 8030 is seen at the yards in Qilidian having arrived light engine to collect the coal train seen alongside. (27 January 2006).

A double westbound departure at the yards in central Pingdingshan. At this time the passenger services were handled by SY Class locomotives while in the background a QJ makes a start with coal empties. (13 April 2004).

Pingzhuang

Pingzhuang Mining Administration in the Mongolian Autonomous Region operates a railway linking several deep coal mines to the national network at Pingzhuang Nan. There was also an opencast mine, which has now closed. SY No. 1017 makes an early morning departure at the servicing point adjacent to the former washery. (24 January 2008).

Two SYs, including smoke deflector-fitted No. 1083, are being prepared for work at the servicing point adjacent to the washery. The loco coal supply is protected from the depredations of the locals by the heavy sliding covers for the storage pit under the grab gantry. (24 January 2008).

The locomotives on this line were very well maintained. SYs No. 1487 and No. 1052 undergo repairs in the gloom of the workshops at Pingzhuang. (24 January 2008).

It was difficult to find where trains were likely to run on the Pingzhuang system and we found SY No. 0400 bringing coal past the Gushan No. 1 Mine purely by chance as we explored the network. (24 January 2008).

Deflector-fitted SY No. 1083 charges across the bridge on the incline towards the China National Railways interchange at Pingzhuang Nan with loaded coal wagons. This is probably the most interesting feature on the whole line. (24 January 2008).

The relatively flat nature of the line is apparent as the coal train approaches the interchange sidings at Pingzhuan Nan. (24 January 2008).

Sandaoling

Having made the long journey to the western deserts of China, it was just after sunrise when I first set eyes upon the Sandaoling Coal Railway, in the Xingyang Autonomous Region, after we turned off the main road and alongside the line that runs to the mines. This JS Class locomotive was running light engine as there were no empties to collect. Before the road and rail split up we stopped, dashed out, and shot a couple of frames before it was gone. Thirty seconds later and we would have missed it. (13 January 2008).

JS No. 8222 pushes a heavy spoil train out of the opencast pit at Sandaoling. The motorcycles belong to the track-repair gang working on the day shift. (15 January 2008).

As well as the opencast pit there are also a couple of deep mines at Sandaoling served by a branch across the desert from Nanzhan. This is the Erjing mine with a JS starting a coal train away from the loading bunker. (16 January 2008).

The empty wagons were always pushed back to the deep mines from the yard at Nanzhan. A JS is on this duty along the branch to the Erjing deep mine. (14 January 2008).

Even though the temperature is below freezing, there is heat haze across the desert as two JS Class locomotives take a train of empty coal wagons to the deep mines at Sandaoling. The Tian Shan mountain range forms a spectacular background on this clear day. (7 December 2009).

It may be sunny but the temperature is well below freezing in the pit. The electric face shovel is loading spoil for removal to distant tips. (13 January 2008).

Sixty-one empty coal wagons and a van, topped and tailed by JS 2-8-2s, are seen slogging uphill across the icy desert from the Liushuguan exchange sidings to Sandaoling. (14 January 2008).

The morning empties again cross the desert with the Tian Shan mountain range as a backdrop. (7 December 2009).

Another morning and JS No. 8366 and JS No. 8358 are thrashing uphill with empties from Liushuguan. All China is on Beijing time and this remote desert area is so far to the west that even at 9.15 a.m. the sun had yet to rise on this cold January morning. (15 January 2008).

JS No. 8053 heads back light engine from the exchange sidings after dropping off a load of full wagons. There were many different photographic opportunities on this line. (11 December 2009).

Level crossings and signs in the opencast coal mine at Sandaoling as a trainload of spoil leaves the pit on a lower line. (13 December 2008).

To exit the lower levels of the opencast pit the spoil trains had to reverse several times as the track zigzagged to gain height. This resulted in trains heading for the tips passing in different directions, as here, where the exhaust steam shows which way they are travelling. (13 January 2008).

Spoil tipping continued twenty-four hours a day and special arrangements had to be made for material to be taken from areas of the opencast pit that were on fire. Darkness falls as another load of spoil is deposited on the burning tip. (15 January 2008).

It was a steep climb up to the high tipping area at Sandaoling. The late evening light is colourful as a spoil train makes the journey. (14 January 2008).

JS No. 8384 undergoing repairs in the Sandaoling loco shed. (16 January 2008).

The workshops at Sandaoling were able to undertake heavy overhauls of the locomotives. In this case, SY No. 1720 is undergoing attention. (16 January 2008).

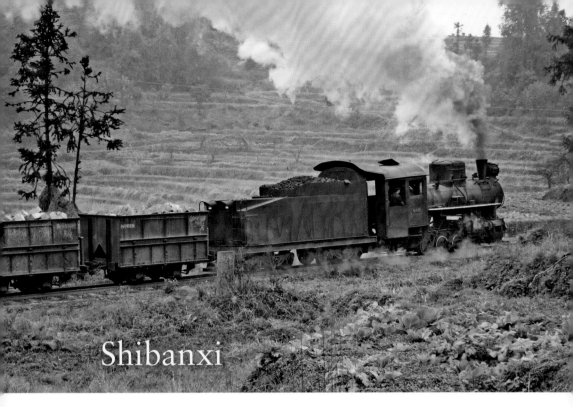

Shibanxi

Freight traffic on the Shibanxi line comprised coal and timber downhill with bricks and gravel for building uphill. Having just left Caiziba, this load of bricks in coal wagons is seen among the vegetables and rice paddies that are typical of this line. (12 December 2008).

A trainload of logs sets off from Mifengyang on the Shibanxi Coal Railway. The timber had been brought down to this place on the backs of a number of pack horses that are used to transport heavy goods in this remote area with no roads. (12 December 2008).

A morning downhill train for Shibanxi is crossing the main road through the village of Yue Jin Qiao where there is a large active coal mine and many blocks of apartments for the workers. The coal is taken down to a power station at Shibanxi using electric locomotives. This scene has now been completely transformed by the construction of new station building to cater for the coachloads of tourists that now come to the line. (9 December 2008).

Even in 2017 it was possible to see freight on this line, although tourist traffic was beginning to predominate. The sun has just crept above the hills as a load of bricks and gravel charges up the bank away from the reversing point at Mifengyang. (13 January 2017).

The introduction of tourist trains has also seen the concept of the 'runpast' being adopted on the curve above Jaioba by trains bound for Bagou. A long viewing platform has been constructed for tourists to stand on while the train is backed across the embankment before returning with whistle and boiler blow-down valve open in an attempt to make a rainbow for the multitude to photograph. (13 January 2017).

The country railway at its best – an afternoon passenger service seen across the rice paddies as it sets off from the stop at the little village of Caiziba. As usual, the carriages look to be well filled with local people. (11 December 2008).

Tiefa

The Diaobingshan (Tiefa) Coal Railway in Liaoning Province comprises a long line from Faku through Diaobingshan to the interchange at Tieling. There was a major junction at Sanjiazi, from where two branches headed off to serve a range of collieries. The network had an intensive passenger service, which made Sanjiazi a busy place at times. Coal trains were sometimes hard to find but here SY No. 1412 was seen when starting a heavy train from a stop at Daqing. (30 September 2004).

A late afternoon passenger departure from Qiaonan heads back towards Sanjiazi. A typical conical spoil tip can be seen beyond the viaduct. (15 April 2005).

Harvest time on the Faku line as SY No. 1749 passes fields of maize being cut. This was a charter train but it proved impossible to persuade the crew to provide some spirited action for the cameras; they were just too professional, and used to using minimum steam and making as little smoke as possible. (1 October 2004).

A passenger train departs Qiaonan Junction for Wangqian on the southernmost branch of the system. The large spoil heaps dominate the coal mining landscape in this area. (15 April 2005).

Its 6.14 a.m. and just daylight as SY No. 1751 hurries a service to Diaobingshan away from Sanjiazi Junction. In the distance is the headgear and spoil heap of the Dalong mine. (16 April 2005).

SY No. 1772, seen south of Wangqian on the Tiefa Coal Railway, was the last standard-gauge steam locomotive built in China, the construction of which was completed in 1999. (14 January 2006).

Once again we see SY No. 1772, this time approaching Diaobingshan with a morning passenger service. The exhaust shows just how cold the winter can be in the north-east of China. (14 January 2006).

The main station at Diaobingshan has three platforms and a distinctive footbridge. Even so, an afternoon departure emerges from under the bridge, having picked up passengers on a non-platform line. (14 January 2006).

Yaojie and Nanlingcheng

In Gansu Province, the Yaojie and Nanlingcheng lines run from the national rail network at Haishiwan serving collieries, power stations, aluminium smelter and an ironworks. They form an end-on junction at Yaojie. On the Nanlingcheng section in Yaojie town, SY No. 1097 climbs to the river bridge, heading for the power station serving the aluminium smelter at Heqiaoyi. (21 January 2006).

In the Yaojie town there are a couple of branches up to the local coal mines that cross a number of the local thoroughfares on the level. SY No. 0527 pushes up to Mine No. 3 and holds up a few shoppers while breakfast dumplings steam on a stove outside a shop. (21 January 2006).

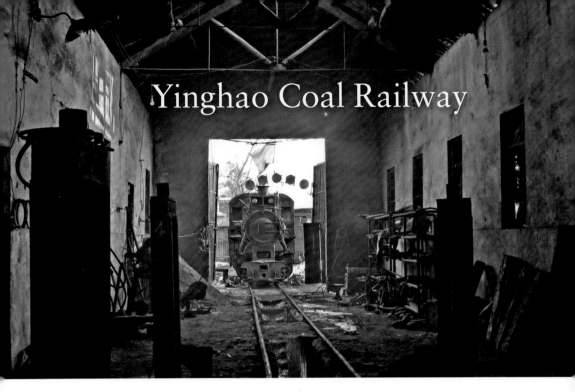

Yinghao Coal Railway

Workshop facilities at the locomotive depot at Yinghaomeikuang were basic, and yet they successfully maintained a fleet of C2 Class locomotives. The locomotive outside has just been fitted with a new cab, which is rather rusty as it has not yet been painted. This line in Henan Province carried coal from collieries at Yinghaomeikuang and Liangjiawajing to the main line at Yinghao. (24 January 2006).

A loaded train is seen here departing the junction at Xiangyang where the traffic was exchanged with the mine branch. Loaded wagons were brought up the steep gradient from the mine three at a time by the locomotive seen on the left. The main line in the background served the workshops at Yinghaomeikuang where the mine had been closed for some time. (24 January 2006).

China is a country of contrasts, such as in this view; a train of empties crosses the motorway on the outskirts of Yinghao, heading back to the collieries. (24 January 2006).

Another train of empties accelerates away from the unloading shed at Yinghao. The gleaners are leaping off with their baskets of coal sweepings as the train gathers speed across the muddy level crossing. (24 January 2006).

The local bus stop is dimly seen through the clouds of steam as a train crosses the main road as it leaves Yinghao. A lot of steam appears to not be reaching the cylinders in this rather run-down C2 Class locomotive. (23 January 2006).

Wreathed in escaping steam, this locomotive dragged three wagons of coal on the approach to the sidings at Xianyang. The brakesman hanging on at the rear looked frozen. (24 January 2006).

Yuanbaoshan

The Yuanbaoshan Mining Railway in the Mongolian Autonomous Region has a long main line linking to the national network at both ends, and there is also a steep branch to a cement works, deep mines and an opencast coal mine. Trains were handled by JS Class locomotives and the passenger services often ran as mixed trains, as here on the viaduct between Gongye and the mine at Fengshuigou. (15 January 2006).

JS No. 6246 shunting in Xizhan yard. The sun was setting on steam operations here as the first diesels were already on order and a conveyor system was due to make a large section of the rail system here redundant. (15 January 2006).

The opencast mine at Yuanbaoshan is only a short distance from the power station as the crow flies, but it is a long way by rail due to a significant difference in height. A conveyor system was constructed with castellated towers where the belt changed directions. For some reason this proved unsuccessful initially and the trains continued for several years. The conveyor provides an unusual background here as JS No. 6246 starts a long and heavy coal train away from the opencast loading bunkers. (23 April 2005).

The bridge over the end of the yard at Yuanbaoshan is a great place to watch the action. On this winter afternoon JS No. 8250 departs with an afternoon mixed service to Fengshuigou while JS No. 8216 waits in the background. (15 January 2006).

JS No. 6544 departs the China National Railways interchange at Yuanbaoshan with a heavy load of coal for the power station in the town. (15 January 2006).

Climbing rapidly from Majiawan and past the cement factory, JS No. 8246 heads for the opencast mine with empty wagons. (15 January 2006).